The Strength of Mercy

Series Preface

The volumes in NCP's "7 x 4" series offer a meditation a day for four weeks, a bite of food for thought, a reflection that lets a reader ponder the spiritual significance of each and every day. Small enough to slip into a purse or coat pocket, these books fit easily into everyday routines.

The Strength of Mercy

Four weeks with Louise de Marillac

Sr. M Veronika Häusler

New City Press
Hyde Park, New York

Published in the United States by New City Press
202 Comforter Blvd., Hyde Park, NY 12538
www.newcitypress.com
©2018 New City Press (English translation)

Cover design by Leandro De Leon
Book design by Belen Velasco
Edited by Maria Blanc
Translated by Marianne Hessing from the original
German *Louise von Marillac, Die Kraft der Barmherzigkeit,
Sr. M. Veronika Häusler*
©2016, Verlag Neue Stadt, München - Zurich - Wien

Library of Congress Cataloging-in-Publication Data:
2017956848

ISBN: 978-1-56548-623-2

Printed in the United States of America

Contents

three

Having a Dauntless Heart –
What Attitudes Help Me Live?

four

Making the World More Human –
What Is My Task?

Louise de Marillac - An Eventful Life

The beginning of Louise's life story holds some question marks - the place of her birth is uncertain, and nothing is known of her mother. Instead, we do know something of her father: Louis is part of the influential de Marillac family. Better known than him are her two uncles: Michel de Marillac (1553-1632), her father's brother, was keeper of the empire's seals; and his half-brother Jean Louis de Marillac, Count of Beaumont (1573-1632), held the post of Marshal of France.

During the 16th and 17th centuries, France went through a phase of armed conflicts, which mostly began as civil war but then turned broader as foreign powers got involved. Torn by civil war and famine, the country lost 30 to 40 percent of its population in those years; the infant mortality rate was at 50 percent, and the average life expectancy for the country folk was 25 years.

Because of her family's ties to the royal court, Louise's life had always been closely linked to the political developments in France.

Her father held the position of captain of the royal bodyguards. His first marriage remained childless, and in 1589 he became a widower. He married again in 1595. Louise had been born out of wedlock in 1591. A few days after her birth, her father claimed her as his daughter and in a notarized document established an annual pension for her. In those days this was uncommon, of course, and suggests that Louis de Marillac was devoted to his daughter with true love. Until his new marriage, she probably grew up with him, but in 1595 she was sent to be educated in the Dominican convent of Poissy. There was no room for her in the new family, even though her father continued to be in close contact with her.

In the convent in Poissy lived her aunt, Catherine Louise de Marillac, a nun; she is believed to be Louise's godmother. The child learned with great talent, and received an education well beyond most of her peers. Literature, Latin and the seven liberal arts all were part of the curriculum, and she also learned to paint. Her childhood ran a rather regular course.

Her father was less fortunate. His second wife brought him into serious financial difficulties, so 12-year-old Louise, apparently for lack of money, had to move into a modest boarding school to live with a spinster. There she acquired new skills such as maintaining a household and doing needlecrafts.

She was not quite 13 years old when her father died in 1604, which was a very painful cut in her life. Now she was in a sense alone in the world, facing an uncertain future. When the very strict religious community of the Daughters of the Passion came to Paris, she decided to join them, with a private vow. However, the provincial refused to accept her - he did not trust that she would be able to lead the hard life of these sisters, because of her weak health. This was another bitter experience of rejection.

Finally, the relatives intervened, and arranged a marriage; the family's background permitted her to look for a decent suitor in the social circles of the Royal Court. The choice fell on Antoine Le Gras, secretary to the Queen. What Louise thought of the marriage and her future husband is not known. The wedding took place on February 5, 1613, at St. Gervais in Paris, and the marriage took on quite well. They moved into an exclusive neighborhood and had their house renovated. On October 18, 1613, their son Michel-Antoine was born.

Soon, however, difficulties started to amount. Their son Michel's development was slow and revealed that the child had special needs - which remained a permanent concern for Louise throughout the coming decades. In the course of political entanglements, the future of the young family was uncertain. Furthermore, in 1617 Louise and her husband also took on the care of seven orphans, the children of an uncle, overstretching their financial capacity significantly. Antoine, her husband, fell ill in 1621; he never did quite recover.

A child with special needs, a sick and difficult husband, financial strains, the care of seven orphans, and Antoine's professional survival threatened by unstable political conditions - these were the hardships Louise found herself in. She became convinced that she was the cause of such disastrous developments, and wrestled with herself whether or not she should leave the family. Yet she could not decide to take that step, as her husband and child depended on her. Despite all her attempts to find help, Louise was ultimately on her own. She came to doubt even the existence of God and for years was trapped in deep despair.

When all hope of overcoming the crisis through well-intended advice, especially from her uncle Michel, led to nothing, God intervened. At least that's how Louise experienced it. On Pentecost 1623 he led her to clearly see the answer to her questions - and he gave her a glimpse into the future. In a community of like-minded people, she would be there for others. This experience, which she calls "light," changed everything for Louise. Outwardly, everything remained as before, but God's direct encouragement pulled her out of the inner night and gave her the strength to consciously accept her circumstances and give shape to her life.

In 1624 or 1625, probably through the intervention of Francis de Sales, Louise came to meet Vincent de Paul, a priest who in 1617 had found-ed the Confraternities of Charity in the French countryside as well as the Association of Caritas ladies in Paris. Vincent became Louise's spiritual director. At first both had felt great reluctance, but then they embarked on a common spiritual journey - another decisive turn in Louise's life. First, however, Antoine's illness worsened, and Louise cared for him and accompanied him until his death on December 21, 1625.

Now she wanted to hasten the fulfillment of the promise; she was impatient. Vincent asked her to live through a time of inner preparation before he accepted her collaboration in 1629. First, she visited the Caritas associations in the countryside, took care of things on site, encouraged the members, gave practical advice, and uncovered shortcomings and developed solutions. Through her extensive training and her practical skills, she was a great help to these associations.

For her as well as for Vincent it was important that both material and spiritual needs were taken care of. So, in their visits they brought supplies of food and clothes and distributed medicines. She taught catechism, especially to the local girls, and trained teachers if there were none at the village. Louise's catechism lessons for women were so popular that the men would hide behind the curtains to listen to her. She even compiled her own catechism.

Now, only one promise of Pentecost remained to be redeemed, the small community of like-minded people, where there would be a coming and going.

Things developed in Louise's favor. In Paris there were problems. The ladies of society who had initially made themselves available for service to the poor in the houses and the Hôtel Dieu, the hospital of the city, could not continue in their task because of family constraints. So they entrusted it to their servants - who showed little enthusiasm for the task at hand.

Providence sent Marguerite Naseau, a young woman who offered herself for service to the poor and motivated other young women to do so. From these beginnings Louise formed the Company of the Daughters of Charity, taking off on November 29, 1633, when four or five young women moved into her house. A year after the foundation Vincent held a conference about the rule Louise had compiled. At that time, there were already twelve sisters.

The needs were great and almost endless. Vincent and Louise had built up a network, and their helpers could be found at all the focal points: in the houses of the poor, as nurses in the hospitals of different cities, in the care for the wounded of the civil wars. Besides that, there was also the care for foundlings and galley slaves. At the request of the Queen of Poland, a former Caritas lady herself, Louise even sent sisters to Warsaw.

As the first superior of the community, she took on the major part of the responsibility for the training of nurses, accompanied them to their assignments, and stayed in touch with them by keeping an extensive correspondence.

On March 25, 1642, Louise and four sisters took the vows of poverty, obedience, chastity, and service to the poor. In the vow formula set down by Louise they promised, "to serve the sick poor, our true Masters" (A. 44b). Thus the promise of Pentecost 1623 finally and fully came true.

Louise's concerns for her son were also alleviated around this time. After Michel had half-heartedly prepared for a clerical career, and ultimately decided against it, he went through some rather wild years. Finally, he found both a suitable position at the royal mint and a good wife. At Louise's deathbed the couple was at her side, together with her granddaughter, Louise Renée.

On March 15, 1660, Louise gave her full life back into the hands of God.

For a long time, March 15 was her feast day.

Since 2016 it has been celebrated on May 9, the day of her beatification in 1920.

Notes on the Translation of the Original Texts

Louise has left extensive writings. Already during her lifetime her secretary, Sr. Marguerite Chetif, recognized the value of her letters, and today we can fall back on the copies kept by Sr. Marguerite, for some of the writings no longer in exist in their original. The Daughters of Charity have tried in ever new attempts to arrange these writings in chronological order, even if no date was specified, and to make them available in French. The first complete edition was published in 1960, followed by a major revision, *Ecrits Spirituels*, in 1983. In it there is a classification of documents. All texts with an "L." before the number are letters. The edition includes 758 of them. An "A." before the number indicates the "thoughts", different writings such as retreat notes, rules, prayers or meditations. In this category there are 88 texts. "M." with a serial number indicates that it is a text from the transcripts of Marguerite Chetif. These include eleven texts.

Louise wrote in the 17th century - and in a sophisticated French. In 1991, *Spiritual Writings of Louise de Marillac*, a complete translation of the French edition of 1983, was published in English by Sr. Louise Sullivan. The English version strives to achieve a careful and faithful translation, while at the same time respecting the concern of using language that is understandable today. The quotations of the original texts in this book draw from this edition.

The respective sources are specified according to common use in *Ecrits Spirituels / Spiritual Writings* as L./A./M. and number specified. Two citations are taken from the "Conferences"[1], conversation logs that were kept at the meetings of the first sisters with Vincent de Paul. Very often these transcripts originate from Louise herself. In the early years, it was common after the death of a sister to speak about her in such a meeting.

---

1. *Pierre Coste (ed.), Saint Vincent De Paul: Correspondence, Conferences, Documents,* Volume I / 1; Volume I / 2, (New City Press, Hyde Park, NY 1985).

Being accepted –
Who am I in the eyes of God?

God's Great Love

Louise's path was full of stumbling blocks - her own difficult family history, challenging political circumstances, the illness of her husband, and her son's developmental problems were part of them just as her own inner afflictions were.

She approached and dealt with them consciously and with honesty and let God come to work in her life. Thus, she gained confidence and trust under his gaze, and accepted the love he showed her. The fruit of letting herself be led was a peaceful acceptance of her own story, thus allowing her to answer with love.

"O admirable love! O hidden secret! What did You want to do, O my God, when You created man since You were not unaware of his weakness? However, the events had to be as they were, O my Master, to make us understand the effects of Your great love."
(A. 13b)

The first book of the Bible speaks of the creation of the world and the human person. Like a refrain it says again and again: "God saw that it was good." This is especially true for human beings: "God saw everything he had made, it was very good" (Gen 1:31).

Louise must slowly grow into this certainty, and this process of growth is marked by much suffering and painful experiences. From the beginning of her life she has to deal with the experience of not being wanted: For the illegitimate child there is no place in the new family of the father; the environment of a monastic community cannot replace a mother's love. Her plan to join a strict religious community fails with the "no" of the priest in charge. After her training in the Household Management School she clearly feels that she is not welcome in her family. The relatives are soon looking for an honorable way to rid themselves of the concern for her by arranging her marriage.

She has to go a long way to realize that God says yes to her, that he has called her into being and intends to do great things with her. She learns to take it seriously that God's wonderful love is meant for *her*.

Louise understands that what she calls "weaknesses", are in fact part of being human - the feeling of alienation and loneliness; the question of whether one's own failure plays a part and distorts the perspective; the experience of falling behind one's own ideals ... All this does not keep God from accepting me as I am, with all that is part of me, that makes me who I am. He desires for me to accept his love - his love which is without limits.

Reflection

- ◎ God gives his yes to me. - I let his commitment take effect in me. What feelings does
  it stir within me?

- ◎ God accepts me as I am. - Do I want to get
  "involved" in this?

The Light of God 2

Louise experiences that God directly answers her questions. She has external afflictions and great inner hardships to endure: the serious illness of her husband, the developmental delay of her son, Michel, the uncertain political situation. With this comes also an inner darkness that leads her to doubt even that there is a God.

"My heart was so depressed that the force of my emotions sometimes resulted in physical pain." (A. 13)

All attempts of human assistance come to nothing; Louise doesn't know anymore where to turn. She wonders whether the difficulties in her family are her own fault, whether it wouldn't be better to leave her husband and son. She does not have a spiritual director anymore and doesn't know how to move in the search for a new one. The abandonment by God she experiences leads her to the brink of desperation. Her affliction becomes unspeakable, the darkness impenetrable - but not so for God: He comes to meet her. Years later, she recalls exactly what she experienced then. This is how she recounts the event of Pentecost 1623:

"On the Feast of Pentecost, during holy Mass or while I was praying in the church, my mind was instantly freed of all doubt ..." (A. 2)

God carefully answers her questions and leads her to find clarity: She shall stay with her husband and be confident regarding the future.

Not least also her painful question for God is answered:

"My third doubt was removed by the inner assurance I felt that it was God who was teaching me these things and that, believing there is a God, I should not doubt the rest."
(A. 2)

This "light," as Louise herself calls the experience, accompanies her for her lifetime. God has shone in her heart. From now on, she knows that he takes her seriously in her searching and questioning and does not leave her alone.

Louise can become encouragement for me, to expose, even in seemingly hopeless situations, my misery with honesty before God - he will give his light also to me.

Reflection

- ◎ Can I voice that which is burdening me with honesty before God?

- ◎ Where did I experience that God takes me seriously and does not leave me alone?

From All Eternity 3

Louise experiences God more directly, as him who is close to her. He wanted to be so close to us that he became man for us in his Son!

Louise writes:

> "God never showed greater love for His creatures than when He resolved to become Man since all the graces that He subsequently bestowed on us depend on this initial act ..."
>
> (A. 7)

She cannot repeat it enough: Everything else depends on the Incarnation. Because God comes to meet the human person, the human person can find God.

> "The Son of God was not satisfied with promising to redeem us or with becoming Man. But He willed to come into this world in a manner not at all consistent with His grandeur. He came as humbly as can be imagined so that we might be more free to approach Him."
>
> (A. 7)

Louise is particularly taken by the fact that God does not come in great power and glory into this world, but as a small, defenseless child. He is born where there is room for him - in a stable.

Without fear or hesitation, the way to him is to be open for all.

In her meditations Louise realizes that the essential motivation for God's action is love.

"The love of God for mankind willed that the son should take human flesh because His delight is to be among His creatures. By becoming like them, He could bear witness to the fact that God has loved them from all eternity. This He did throughout His human life upon earth." (A. 27)

God cannot express any more clearly how much the human person means to him - how much I mean to him. He wants me to come to him with all that I am and all that I have - without fear, without hesitation, with great trust.

Reflection

◎   Do I allow God to come closer to me?

◎   How can I meet him?

Life in Abundance

In God's creation, the human person has a special place. Louise writes:

> *"I thought that man is the chief work of God's creative power."* (A. 22)

She learns to accept the greatness of man in God's eyes - and her own greatness - and so grows into a liberating gratitude towards God.

Nevertheless, the experience remains that this relationship is disturbed again and again; that the free view at the loving God is blocked. Louise sees the reason for this in sin, in all the aspects of behavior that are not according to God, that are contrary to the confidence in him. Sin separates, interrupts the flow of security and strength. She recognizes *"that sin had, in a way, nullified this work by preventing the creature from rejoicing in his God"* (A. 22).

When the relationship between God and man is undimmed, it is characterized by joy: the person finds joy in his or her being, in others, and in the world that surrounds them. *This* is what God wants for man; this is - as the Old Testament says - "Shalom," or, as Jesus puts it in the Gospel of John: "life in abundance" (cf. Jn 10:10).

If this bond is disturbed by sin, it is painfully felt not only by man. This being an active relationship, God also feels the interruption. Louise is very sensitive and delicate; she strongly perceives the moments when this free flow of love is blocked. However, she experiences just as clearly that God always comes towards her to meet her and reconnect the thread.

"God did not intend this separation to be permanent. Therefore, this same God, Father, Son and Holy Spirit, who had said: "Let us make man to our image and likeness," now resolved to create him anew by redeeming him." (A. 22)

To return to God, to return home to the security with him, to be able to leave behind everything that divides, that is truly the experience of being created anew.

Reflection

◎   Do I look with joy at my life, my fellow human beings, my environment, God?

◎   Is there currently something that "interrupts" the connection with God? I bring it before him ...

A New Creation

God comes towards the human person and makes him or her able to live life as a "new creation" (cf. 2 Cor 5:17), centered on Christ. Louise's answer is the irrevocable willingness to follow him and to live according to the model of his life, his thoughts, and his actions. She writes to a fellow sister:

"It is only reasonable that those whom God has called to follow His Son should strive to become holy as He is holy and to make their lives a continuation of His." (L. 328)

It is from the Gospel that this looking at Christ is nourished. In the Gospel she discovers how he encounters people and acts in these encounters, the spirit that animates him. In Louise's writings and letters, we see in detail how she is able to enter into the life and thoughts of Jesus; everything that happens in her everyday life, every experience and encounter brings her in contact with him.

Three examples:

Praying at the crib encourages her to be like Jesus himself, merciful in contact with other people, loving and uncomplicated, so that it becomes easy to reach out to them. (cf. A. 8)

*When she moves to a new home, she re-
solves "by this change of residence, to honor
the changes made by Jesus and the Blessed
Virgin when they moved from Bethlehem to
Egypt and then to other places, not wanting,
any more than they, to have a permanent
dwelling here on earth." (A. 15)*

*When she thinks about the events at Easter,
she feels the "desire to rise with our Lord."
It is clear to her that Jesus had to go through
dying and death to enter into new life. She
realizes "that it is my evil inclinations which
must die" (A. 12), so that new life is possible.*

When I feel this close relationship between
my life and the life of Jesus, I can make Louise's
resolution my own:

*"Filled with consolation and happiness at the
thought of being accepted by Him to live my
entire life as His follower, I resolved that in
everything, particularly in uncertain or ques-
tionable circumstances, I would consider
what Jesus would have done." (A. 5)*

Reflection

◎ Connect the experiences of my day with
the experience of Jesus ...

◎ Ask him: What would you do in my place?

Compassionate Guidance 6

Under God's loving gaze Louise recognizes that, despite all that is broken and all the difficulties, it is precisely in her own life story that she can find God. His compassionate guidance, which leads her step by step, makes her write:

"God, who has granted me so many graces, led me to understand that it was His holy will that I go to Him by way of the Cross. His goodness chose to mark me with it from my birth and He has hardly ever left me, at any age, without some occasion of suffering." (A. 29)

Louise does not embellish her story; she calls the way God led her, "cross". However, neither does she remain defensive nor does she give in to resignation - she recognizes that from the stumbling blocks which over a long period have marked her own story, she can build something unique: her life. At the basis of this is the experience that she is not left alone. God guides her and provides in the person of St. Vincent de Paul a reliable companion at her side.

From accepting herself, she gradually reaches reconciliation and acceptance of her story, as it is uniquely hers. Louise understands that God's providence accompanies the whole journey and makes everything for the good - as difficult as it may seem in actual experience. This experience lets her exclaim:

"Since grace had many times enabled me to esteem and desire this state, I trusted that His goodness would, again today, grant me a new grace to carry out His holy will. I begged Him, with all my heart, to place me in this state no matter how painful I found it" (A. 29).

Louise teaches us: Deep trust in God, and faith in his mercy which embraces all brokenness and heals it, make reconciliation possible.

Keeping our gaze on Christ, who as man has become our brother and walks at our side, brings all our restlessness and fear to a halt and leads our pain towards peace.

Reflection

◎   Does my life hold anything broken, that I cannot (yet) accept?

◎   Where is there a need for reconciliation?

Dialogue of Love

"Yes, You truly love us since You are one with the Father, who willed to show us His love by giving us You, His only Son. We are also certain that You want us to love you. Both Your old and Your new law command us to do so." (A. 27)

As she walks the path of her life, Louise comes to know God as the one who comes to meet her, who accepts her and says yes to her. Since in Jesus Christ he has lived the human condition with all its facets, he is present in everything that makes up human life.

He knows how joy and gratitude feel, he knows enthusiasm and passion. Just as he has experienced rejection and resistance, sadness, fear and loneliness. He has loved and struggled, has had to overcome failures and bring about reconciliation.

This is the greatest gift, the greatest grace: that he is simply there.

He is there for me and with me. Louise is overwhelmed by it: *"You really love us."*

She feels that this declaration of love in which God comes to her, reaches out for an answer: *"... you want us to love you."*

It is about a dialogue of love, which in this way can develop between God and the human person and brighten and broaden life. So she continues:

"O power of love! O admirable treasure hidden in the depths of the soul! O excellence of the creature who knows You! All mankind would take delight in it." (A. 27)

Love has its place in the innermost depth of the heart, in the "depths of the soul" - and pushes to the outside. The joy of being able to feel the love of God wants to spread, contaminate, set sparks. It develops an irresistible force that does not see any more obstacles.

"O pure love, how I love you! Since You are as strong as death, separate me from all that is contrary to you." (A. 27)

Reflection

◎ Can I accept God's love?

◎ How do I react to the realization: *"You really love us?"*

Looking to God
Who is God for me?

two

Louise's relationship with God develops over the course of her life. At first, God is of unimaginable great majesty for her; she addresses him in rather abstract terms. With time, she comes to know a God who is mercifully close to her, who carefully guides her and lets himself be found right there in everyday life.

Keeping her gaze fixed on the Triune God becomes precious for her and motivates her to continually strive for unity in diversity. From the experience of the Pentecost event, life in the light of the Holy Spirit takes on a great significance for her.

Increasingly though, the heart of her spirituality is the gaze at Christ, on which she consistently centers her life. Thus, she comes to find union with God.

Life to the Full

Every active relationship changes over time and grows through manifold experiences, matures in crises and enriching encounters, and so also Louise's relationship with God changes throughout her life.

Through her intense and thorough studies, she had developed great clarity of mind and had learned to think systematically. This also forms her concept of God. She tries to capture the greatness of God through reason; her spiritual life is nourished greatly from the insights she gains through reflection and contemplation.

In that way, her piety initially leads her to very abstract statements about God:

"In the one true being of God resides the essence of all the other beings which, in His goodness, He has created." (A. 24)

God for her is the Great, the Majestic, the Infinite.

In the time of her dark night Louise experiences how incomprehensible and difficult the work of God may feel in one's own life. Yet precisely during this time something new breaks open in her that enables her to find a much more direct and wholesome experience of God. She does not avoid her interior darkness – and in that way God becomes always more a "counterpart" for her. She experiences that he knows her, knows her innermost sentiments, and takes her seriously.

With that, the greatness of God takes on a new meaning for her. All that is good, all the virtues, all the graces are in God; the human person can come and draw from this infinite source. God wants to give himself to the human person, to let him or her share in his fullness. Therefore, Louise recognizes the goal with a new clarity: to be person in front of God is to understand his intentions, and to receive his grace. She writes in a retreat reflection:

"The infinite goodness and wisdom of God leave the soul free to draw on the infinite sources of His love." (A. 7)

God gives life to the full. Our dealing with him should be characterized by freedom and trust. We are invited to draw from God's wealth.

Reflection

◉   What shapes my concept of God?

◉   What images do I have of him?

Trinitarian Unity

The God who is becoming always more a living counterpart in Louise's life, who increasingly fills her thoughts, feelings and actions, is in himself a God of relationship. Louise reflects intensely on the mystery of the Trinity. Twice a day she turns in prayer to the Holy Trinity:

> "I adore You, Most Holy Trinity, one God in three Persons, and I thank You for all the graces that, in Your goodness, You have bestowed upon me." (A. 49b)

For her the Trinity, the exchange between Father, Son, and Holy Spirit, is the place where redemption has its beginning. Louise uses the image of the Trinity in convening a council meeting.

> "As soon as human nature had sinned, the Creator, who wanted to repair this fault by a great act of pure love, ordered, in the Council of His Divinity, that one of the three Persons should become Man.
> But, my soul, what is God asking of us by the Incarnation of His dear Son other than gratitude for our Redemption?" (A. 7)

The one God is in himself relationship, and desires relationship, and therefore the human person, created anew by God through redemption, is the image of God also in the sense that he or she is created as communitarian in nature. He or she is called to create anew the reality of one's life by one's actions - in relationship with God, but also in dealing with each other.

Thus, the reflection on the Trinity has a very practical aspect for Louise. The people she works with come from very different backgrounds Apart from the Daughters of Charity, who are mostly young women from rural areas, there are also the aristocratic ladies of Parisian society; the Confraternities of Charity in the rural parishes speak and think differently than the town counselors in big cities like Angers, with whom she must negotiate contracts. It is Louise's concern to respect them all in their diversity, without allowing these differences to become a source of division. Her guiding principle is the unity in the Trinity, as the following advice shows:

"They shall honor the Blessed Trinity by great union among themselves. This union shall be neither constrained nor forced but always maintained by gentle necessity which cordiality transforms into mutual affection." (A. 38)

Reflection

◎ What do I associate with the Mystery of the Trinity?

◎ What is important to me in relationships?

For God Alone

God has called the human person to life out of love, and in redemption created us anew. Louise recognizes that this certainty of her faith applies to her personally. In awe, she confesses:

"The Triune God, in the unity of His essence, created me for Himself alone. He has loved me from all eternity. Seeing that I could neither come into being nor subsist without Him, since He is my first and only origin, He wants also to be my end and, indeed, He must be." (A. 19)

She knows that she can mature into the joyous breadth of the relationship with the Triune God and have an unconditional trust in his providence. As she often writes, his providence, the intention God has for her life, is the golden thread leading through her life.

She is convinced: God finds ways and means to share of himself with the human person. He does this in a profound delicateness, waiting for our free consent. When after her husband's death she formulates a "Rule of life in the world" for herself, she resolves:

"Upon awakening, may my first thought be of God. May I make acts of adoration, thanksgiving and abandonment of my will to His

most holy will. Reflecting on my lowliness and powerlessness, I shall invoke the grace of the Holy Spirit in which I shall have great confidence for the accomplishment of His will in me, which shall be the sole desire of my heart." (A. 1)

The certainty that God's will is found in everyday occurrences, and her resolution to put herself at his disposal, enable her to mobilize her strength – in an amazing measure, given her delicate constitution. In her faith, she is certain that God will make everything work for good. She does not tire of winning over those who are at work with her to be docile to God's intentions:

"Let us always adore and love the guidance of Divine Providence, the true and only security of the Daughters of Charity." (L. 201)

Reflection

◎ Do I allow myself to be led?

◎ Do I trust God, that he wants what is best for me?

I Desire It Thus

The experiences of her life, especially the experience of the Pentecost event, let her come to the certainty that God carries her life and that his will healingly leads her.

But she does not in any way lose the awareness that his will at times is not easy to carry. Keeping her eyes fixed on Jesus Christ is decisive for her. Just as Jesus accepted the will of the Father and in order to redeem us did not avoid the cross, so Louise declares herself ready to accept the adversities of her life, and to understand them as a way to bring her closer to him.

"Let us take the first step in following Him which is to exclaim, I desire it thus, my dear Spouse, I desire it thus. As proof thereof, I am going to follow you to the foot of Your Cross ... At the foot of this holy, sacred and adored Cross, I sacrifice everything that might prevent me from loving." (A. 27)

From this perspective Louise can take upon herself the difficulties of her own life and deal with them in a reconciled way. At the same time, she looks beyond herself and with the alertness of her heart senses where she can help others to carry their cross.

In this, Louise is in no way a defender of a mystic's suffering. For her it is rather about accepting suffering where, in accepting the will of God, this suffering is unavoidable, and therefore, having the good sense to do whatever helps to better the situation. Thus, she encourages a sick sister:

"My very dear Sister, Our God is truly making you a participant in His suffering by permitting you to be seriously ill. ... Rest assured that it is a sign of God's love for you since it is through this that He makes you somewhat like His Son. Suffer then, in His same spirit. ...and use every means given to you to recover your health." (L. 88)

Reflection

- ◎ How do I react when I have to deal with difficult matters?

- ◎ What approach do I have to Christ and his Cross?

Darkness Dispersed 5

During her schooling in the Cloister of Poissy, Louise learns to paint.

The painting in which she depicts the "Lord of Mercy", and which presently can be seen in the Motherhouse of the Daughters of Charity in Paris, may appear strange today in its representation. It can convey though, more than any words, how Louise saw and understood Christ.

She comes to know who Jesus Christ is by meditating on the Holy Scriptures. Three aspects which are most important to her are captured in this painting:

There is first the *attitude* which Christ displays. In it, God's coming to meet us is expressed, which deeply stirs Louise. It is an attitude of listening, of mindfulness, of care. His gaze is all attentiveness. At the same time, Jesus is listening within.

In his expression lies a decisiveness and at the same time a peaceful serenity. Christ knows where he wants to go, and yet he lets himself be affected by people or circumstances he encounters; he remains the gentle one.

Then the gaze falls onto *the open heart*. The motivation for the Son in taking on humanity and sharing in it in all its facets, is what Louise calls "pure love." We have once and for all gained access to this love. Nothing can separate us from the love of Christ. Confidently we can entrust ourselves to God in the assurance that all darkness is dispersed, gathered into the luminescence of this opened heart.

Just as Christ has us at heart, he invites us in turn to open our hearts to those whom we encounter; we ourselves are called upon to take the risk of "the open heart."

The third message is conveyed by the *open hands*. With such opened hands, the dynamics of receiving and giving become possible.

Christ stretches out his hands to us; the nail-marks are visible. The love of Christ, Louise reminds us, is a love which knows suffering.

Christ's hands are an invitation to engage in the encounter with him, to draw close to him. Being a Christian is before all else a call to be close to him, an invitation to come and see, to stay and to search in everyday occurrences the connection with him.

Louise reminds us thus:

> *"Since, at the creation of the world, God taught us that our resemblance to Him was dependent on His love. Let us preserve this image within us by means of two eminent perfections: purity and charity. ...*
> *Therefore, let us love this love and we will thereby grasp its endlessness since it depends in no way on us. Let us often recall all the*

actions of the life of our Beloved so that we may imitate them." (A. 27)

Reflection

◎ What connection do I find to this picture?

◎ How does Christ touch me in this depiction - in his coming towards me, in the gaze at his open heart, through his opened hands?

6 The Great Feast

Under the impression of the Pentecost event of 1623, Louise cultivates a special relationship with the Holy Spirit and lives the Feast of Pentecost, which she herself calls "the great Feast," with special attention. Every year between Ascension Day and Pentecost she holds a retreat and reflects on this deep experience, that on Pentecost Day the Holy Spirit with his light illumined her inner night and the pressing question of her vocation.

"It is true that I have a special affection for the feast of Pentecost and this time of preparation for it is very dear to me." (L. 118b)

She establishes in the Rule that the sisters, if possible, should use the time between Ascension Day and Pentecost to honor the communion of Mary and the apostles, who in their loss of the visible presence of Jesus are awaiting the Paraclete in inner recollection (cf. A. 75).

For Louise, the Holy Spirit stands in close relationship with God's providence – in his light God's providence can be recognized.

His strength lets us interpret our experiences from God's perspective. His fire enflames in us the readiness to put ourselves at his disposal, and to use our gifts in his service. Louise urges us to pray that Christ may send his Holy Spirit,

"that we may be so filled with His Spirit that we may do nothing or say nothing except for His glory and His holy love." (L. 345)

In the Holy Spirit Louise sees the strength that allows her to overcome her own limitations since he is the Spirit of the Risen One, who has overcome death and darkness once and for all. Thus, she can pray:

"O Eternal Light, lift my blindness! ... Humble my heart to receive Your graces. ... May the power to love which You have placed in my soul no longer stop at the disorder of my self-sufficiency which, in reality, is but powerlessness and an obstacle to the pure love which I must have as a result of the indwelling of the Holy Spirit." (A. 26)

Reflection

◉ Have I ever experienced how God unexpectedly intervened and guided the course of events?

◉ Which gift do I especially ask the Holy Spirit for?

7 Continuous Remembrance

In her prayers and recollections and in her service for others Louise matures into unity with God.

"It seems to me that our interior conversation with God should consist in the continuous remembrance of His holy presence." (M. 73)

She keeps this continuous remembrance in whichever mood she finds herself. Also, difficult moments, when they are accepted in union with God, can further the unity with him and become reason for gratitude:

"On all those occasions which are painful to our senses, we must consider the paternal goodness of God. ... Let us therefore, make acts of thanksgiving." (M. 73)

Of course, not only painful events – joy and successful undertakings also lead to a greater closeness to God:

"When pleasant things happen to us or when our undertakings succeed as we wish them to, before abandoning ourselves to the joy of the moment, let us glance interiorly toward God and thank Him for His mercy since it is

His love alone which affords us this consolation." (M. 73)

Louise remains realistic – she knows that inner peace and stillness of the heart are always under new attack:

"Sometimes we are under pressure, and it seems to us that we urgently need and hope for help from others. However, we are disappointed. This happens either through the conduct of Divine Providence or because of human weakness. We must then look immediately to the will of God and accept it in this situation. We should raise our minds to God, and depend only on Him, remembering that, from all eternity, He has been and is sufficient to Himself; consequently He can and should be sufficient for us." (M. 73)

To find God in every situation of our daily life, in every stirring of the heart, and to be certain, that his love and his presence suffice for everything to turn for the good – that is what Louise invites us to.

Reflection

◎   When do I look for God – in difficulties, in success, when I am happy?

◎   Can I say from my heart with full conviction: "God is enough"?

Having a Dauntless Heart
– Which attitudes help me live?

three

Sharing All with Christ

"The only means for me to find the mercy of God [at the hour of my death] is to have, at that moment, the image of Jesus Christ imprinted upon my soul." (A. 8)

This title shows Louise's guiding image: the gaze at Christ, from whom she learns. His contacts with others form her way of encountering people and being at their side. His being one with God inspires her prayer life. He can be close to her because he is fully human himself, and thus is present in our reality. For Louise this experience of intense closeness turns into certainty, when one morning she sets out on a trip to visit the Caritas associations:

"I left on the Feast of St. Agatha, February 5, to go to Saint-Cloud. At the moment of Holy Communion, it seemed to me that Our Lord inspired me to receive Him as the Spouse of my soul and that this communion was a manner of espousal. I felt myself more closely united to Him ..." (A. 50)

Louise uses the image of spousal communion of goods. Everything that happens to her she regards as common possession.

Sharing everything with Christ; whatever I experience, each joy, every difficulty; live it together with him in the certainty that he knows what I am speaking about – that is how with Louise we can describe "following Christ." It becomes clear that "the image of Christ" she speaks about, is not something static, but the shared reality of her life. Thus, for Louise an exchange develops that makes her happy and leads her to the conscious decision to fully engage in life with Christ.

"Because Jesus took our misery upon Himself, it is only reasonable that we should follow Him and imitate His holy, human life. This thought absorbed my mind and moved me to resolve to follow Him wholeheartedly, without any reservations." (A. 5)

Reflection

- ◎ How do I feel about the realization that everything I live belongs to both Jesus and myself?

- ◎ Which reality of my life do I share concretely today with Jesus Christ?

Humility

Louise's letters and writings very often speak of a triad of attitudes, which in her view make a successful life possible: *humility, simplicity,* and *love*. These characteristics may sound unfamiliar and bulky in today's world, so that an attentive ear is needed for us to understand what Louise wants to express.

There is first of all *humility*.

It has become clear that Louise is deeply moved by God's coming to us so much so as to become man in his Son. In it she sees fully realized what she calls "humility": that God gives up the inviolability of his glory and enters into our reality.

What does that mean for Louise?

"I must practice interior humility by a desire for abjection and exterior humility by willingly accepting all the occasions which occur for humbling myself. I shall do this in order to honor the true and real humility of God Himself in whom I shall find the strength to overcome my pride, to combat my frequent outbursts of impatience and to acquire charity and gentleness toward my neighbor. Thus I shall honor the teaching of Jesus Christ who told us to learn of Him to be gentle and humble of heart." (A. 7)

For Louise it is part of humility to be truthful to oneself. This means to look with honesty at one's own ways of acting and being, and at one's motivations. God's loving gaze lets Louise recognize where she has to overcome what is not good, and where she has to grow further into the good.

Moreover, humility has very practical consequences for living with one another. It concerns the way of approaching the other, of asking rather than demanding, of being grateful also for things that are seemingly taken for granted, of being patient.

Humility makes itself felt as a high regard for the dignity of the others an attitude, which; in a profound way makes us become sensitive. Louise feels with the other and does not remain untouched by his or her joy or suffering.

Humility lets us recognize what the other person needs, how I can serve him or her with my talents, my presence, my time.

Humility therefore, is not at all an attitude that makes one small or bending to the other, but one that is attentive to how life can develop.

Therefore, if there are difficulties in living with one another, Louise is convinced:

"True humility will regulate everything."
(L. 11)

Reflection

- ◎   Does the word humility mean anything to me? Can I commit to Louise's views?

- ◎   What does this attitude mean for me concretely in my environment?

Simplicity

The second attitude of the triad, of which Louise speaks, also sounds a little peculiar at first. The French original uses the word *simplicite*. It is translated usually as *simplicity* or *simple-ness.*

Louise intends with it an attitude that tries to look at things or situations as much as possible undisguised, and avoids being complicated.

This holds true, for example, in the relationship with God: Because he comes to us, we can be fully undisguised before him.

In Matthew's Beatitudes it says: "Blessed are the pure of heart, for they shall see God." (Mt 5:8)

I am invited to look for him with an open heart, and to find him in everything I live and perceive.

To a lady to whom she gives spiritual guidance, Louise writes:

"Speak to our Lord with great simplicity and innocent familiarity. Do not be concerned whether or not you experience any consolation; God wants only our hearts." (L. 40)

This immediacy of God becomes for Louise a source of personal unambiguity and transparency. Her convictions and motivations become visible through all her speaking and acting. She can encounter those around her with great clarity and coherence.

That is where with great emphasis she leads also the young women entrusted to her. In a social environment which is strongly marked by class differences, they are not seldom tempted to procure a position for themselves and a certain recognition. Louise stands in her conviction: The dignity of a person and the esteem he or she deserves are independent of all the external attributes. So, it is necessary to look with honesty at what inner forces I am propelled by.

"I urge them to dispose themselves to make their communications truthfully and with simplicity of heart, for the glory of God ..." (L. 640)

The attitude of simplicity as Louise understands it indicates that the knowledge of one's own dignity bestowed on us by God is the way to develop a realistic image of oneself, to learn to stand by oneself in truthfulness, and to be upright in dealings with others.

Reflection

◉   Can I be honest before God?

◉   How important is it for me to receive recognition and esteem from others? Do I stand by my own person?

Love 4

The third attitude, which is so important for Louise, is *love*. She is aware that all human love is an answer to God's love for us. She knows that God with his love is residing in her, remains in her, and has his home in her. This for her is mandate and motivation to freely give of this treasure, to allow others to become at home in this love.

The experiences of her life have made her become a very sensitive and compassionate woman. The sisters who have lived with her, describe her as attentive to obvious and hidden needs, and as cordial and courteous. That is how she is with everyone: her family, her community, the poor, the sick, and foundlings who are entrusted to her. In an exchange after her death the sisters recount:

> *"She had a great love for the poor, and when there was the opportunity, she served them with great joy. She was exceedingly kind and helpful with all the Sisters, always bearing with and excusing them. Whenever it was necessary though, she also knew how to correct with strictness. But also that, she did out of love: because she had a sympathetic heart for all those who were suffering physi-*

*cally or spiritually. She also was able to pa-
tiently tolerate sisters for years who because
of their faults should have been sent away.
She always waited to see, if they would not
improve."* (Conferences I/2, The Virtues of
Mademoiselle Louise de Marillac, July 3rd,
1660)

So became of the word love a colorful bou-
quet of very practical manners: goodness, help-
fulness, patience, forbearance, clarity, empathy,
the gift of differentiation, faith in possibilities to
develop ...

Reflection

◎   Where do I experience love?

◎   Which "flowers" can I contribute to the
     bouquet?

Esteem and Cordiality 5

Another characteristic pair of attitudes, which we find in Louise, are *esteem and cordiality*. She writes to the sisters in Paris:

"All my dear Sisters, I greet you affectionately and beg you, for the love of our dear Master, Jesus Crucified, to work well toward your perfection ... through the cordiality and respect you owe one another, and through the edification you must give one another in all your words and actions." (L. 193)

Louise is deeply convinced that every relationship has to be marked by esteem and respect for the other, because of the unalienable dignity given by God. However, this esteem could also become impersonal, and lead to a reservedness in which the other always remains a stranger. Therefore, Louise strives to give esteem a partner at her side: cordiality. She notes from a "Conference", which Vincent gave to the sisters:

"My daughters, you should first of all know, that there are two ways to show each other respect. The first is more serious and measured, the other one cordial and gentle. The first one, respect, has often something forced

about, subordinates keep it in front of their superiors: at times it is more the result of fear than of good intention, and so it neither comes from the heart nor is it authentic. The respect that you, my daughters, owe each other, always has to be accompanied by real cordiality, making it a true show of respect, as the angels have for each other." (Conferences I/1, Cordial Respect, January 1st, 1644)

When esteem and cordiality characterize people's living together, this can help to overcome many difficulties and bring consolation and relief in many a hardship.

Louise is convinced that the bond which thus develops is resilient and opens that space needed for the other to know they are accepted and secure.

Thus, it is for her a sign of a credible decision for one's own vocation that those who commit to this way, *"show great cordiality and give proof of strong and respectful friendship."* (A. 63)

Reflection

◎ Which characteristics mark my relationships – in the family, in my friendships, in my profession?

◎ Where do I experience resilient support – and where can I give it?

Inner Joy

The attitudes which Louise in her journey discovers as helpful in life, attitudes which she lives and tries to further in others, lead into a great breadth and freedom of the heart, and therefore not least to a lightness and joy.

Her gaze is turned in all directions: The sisters shall be happy, that they can correspond to the will of God; the poor shall be happy, because God's mercy becomes tangible for them. Yes, even God himself shall be happy, when he sees how those who let themselves be called and guided by him do their service with open hearts.

With this Louise assumes that joy is a fruit of abandoning oneself to God's guidance and handing oneself over to his will. She writes:

> *"I sacrifice everything that might prevent me from loving, with all the purity that You expect of me, without ever aspiring to any other joy than submission to Your good pleasure and to the laws of Your pure love." (A. 27)*

Out of this clarity grows an indestructible inner joy. Louise is a master at recognizing where joy is hidden, if only we are aware of it. A little taste:

- ◎ *"You must believe, my dear Sisters, that noth-ing gives me greater joy than to learn about each one of you, about your health and about your interior dispositions ..." (L. 468)*

- ◎ *"You made me very happy by standing firm ..." (L. 640)*

- ◎ *"You pleased me greatly by reminding me ..." (L. 620)*

- ◎ *"I admit that I am wrong and that it has been too long since I have allowed myself the consolation of writing to you. You give me great pleasure by not holding that against me ..." (L. 634)*

- ◎ *"We would really like you to send us a good supply of codfish, one which can be transported and kept easily." (L. 293)*

Louise knows that joy cannot be "created." Attentiveness, of course, can contribute to discovering joy; refraining from brooding over things can prepare the way to achieving it.

Nonetheless, joy ultimately is and remains a gift that must be prayed for.

"I advise you to ...ask the Holy Spirit for joy, which is one of His seven gifts." (L. 102)

Reflection

◎ What do I rejoice about?

◎ How does my daily life change, when I discover in little things reasons for being joyful?

7 An Undaunted Heart

In 1645 two sisters are sent to a place where they find a difficult situation: An excessive workload is awaiting them; moreover they also meet rejection and resistance. To the two of them she writes:

"Be so stout-hearted that you find nothing difficult for the most holy love of God and of His crucified son ..." (L. 344)

This wish expresses an attitude which shines through in all of her encounters: encouragement.

Louise knows that difficulties and opposition are part of life. To overcome them successfully, it takes an "undaunted," a wide, an unperturbable heart. Thus, she points out that great inner dimension is necessary in the single person, openness and the readiness to commit to what lies ahead. She writes:

"Let us be more courageous, my dear Sisters, and let us accomplish, insofar, as we are able, the words God addressed to His Son ... May this come about through the effect of Jesus' words when He promised that He would draw all to Himself when He was lifted up." (A. 27)

If we walk in Louise's footsteps, we see that this openness and availability at times will demand a lot of us; but we shall not be afraid of that. Louise urges us to have an "undaunted heart," to approach with spiritedness, bravery, strength, impetus, energy, and fearlessness the tasks entrusted to us. Cooperation in God's plans, in mankind, and the world becoming whole, is worth this price.

She finds the key to approaching things the right way in delicately sensing where strengths and limits are lying – in herself and in others. She is convinced: the strongpoints are gaining strength, if they are put at the service of a vision, if they don't let themselves be restrained by the seemingly impossible, but if by patiently sticking to our inner conviction we stand up undeterred for the fulfillment of our ideals. In this Louise moves, and we move with her, in the footsteps of Jesus, who remained faithful to his mission – up to giving up his life. The love of Jesus Christ goes with us through all the ups and downs, and is the true empowerment to living with a dauntless heart.

Reflection

◎   How do I approach challenges?

◎   For which vision, which ideal, do I make myself strong?

Making the world
more human
What is my task?

four

Our journey in faith, following him, carries with it a strong impulse for Louise. She wants to give her contribution, so that the world may change for the good. She is convinced: God calls everyone to a specific task; every effort has value and is indispensable. The human person grows from a dynamic of listening to "God's intention" and the inner readiness to be available. Louise discovers in this the fulfillment of her life and encourages us to decisively walk our own path.

Mercy, Undeserved and in Rich Measure

Louise's commitment to others with their manifold concerns and afflictions is rooted in the strength of mercy, draws from its resilient strength and becomes fruitful in an impressive way.

She sees mercy as a dynamic which comes from God and which God wants to come through her to others. It is anchored in the fact that she experiences in ever new ways how he shows her his mercy undeserved and in rich measure. Thus, she resolves:

"O my God, I wish to reflect often upon this and to recognize Your infinite mercy because You created me." (A. 14b)

This experience of the love of God, this coming to know who he really is, urges her to be loving and merciful herself. As is characteristic for Louise, the insight leads to a resolution:

"I want to do everything in my power to practice this Holy Love." (A. 29)

On this basis a force-field develops in which each person receives what is due to him or her in God. This eases also the much-discussed tension between mercy and justice.

Naturally that turns the usual order of things on its head. For Louise those whom she assists, "are our masters and we must love them tenderly and respect them deeply." (L. 284b)

In ever new ways merciful love makes her creative: be it in procuring professional help for the sick, in creating a life-advancing atmosphere for the foundlings, in making use of the means of the Caritas clubs in appropriate ways and through good organization, or in carefully accompanying those who are searching. Louise's commitment contributes to the fact that the realities of people's lives are changing.

She is always reminded of where her strength stems from: "This leads me to hope in His divine mercy." (A. 5)

Reflection

◎ Which images – notions – sentiments do I associate with "mercy"?

◎ Where can I contribute in my environment so that people receive what is due to them from God?

Sharing in Solidarity

Louise would probably bring the realization of mercy to the point with a short expression: *Service*. By serving she and her companions live up to their mission:

> *"O, how evident it is that God loves you since He provides you with so many opportunities to serve Him! Continue to do so, I beg of you, for love of Him, with all the gentleness, concern and charity required of you." (L. 468)*

Not just in our day does speaking of service have an unpleasant aftertaste – already in Louise's time she had to help her sisters to rediscover the *dignity of serving*.

Essential in her understanding of serving is that our actions and attention are more than mere services, which each sister must perform; rather the approach lies in the relationship between her and *God*. In God every human being, herself included, is first of all a person who is simultaneously needy, gifted by God, and receiving – out of his free will God serves the human person, even the one who himself or herself is serving.

> *"His benign gaze protects the grace which subsists in us by His love and goodness*

*alone. Therefore, I must be eternally grateful
to Him for this as well as for His mercy which
He shows us in all the actions of His holy life
…" (A. 42)*

This requires openness and receptiveness on
our part, acknowledging one's own dependence:
only when I accept that I can be needy myself
and that I am held, can I healingly turn towards
others and their needs. Too great otherwise
would be the temptation to overstrain myself and
to overestimate my own abilities.

In this perspective serving becomes a sharing
in solidarity, an encounter at eye level, a chance
to encounter Christ in the other person, and one's
actions are characterized by spontaneous attention without reservations towards anyone who
needs help. Louise's example challenges us to
"invest" ourselves in our encounters with others,
to advocate for their rights and their dignity, and
to use the gifts, talents and skills entrusted to us.
Then we can do our service *"thanking God for
the grace which He has given to us in calling us
to serve Him in the person of the poor"* (A. 75).

Reflection

◎ Does the word "service" even exist in my
vocabulary?

◎ Whom do I serve? How does this change
me?

A Spirit of Unity 3

Early in her youth Louise already knows how to enthuse others for a common cause. As a young girl she convinces her classmates in the Household Management School to make and sell crafts to bolster the community fund.

As soon as she becomes a collaborator of Vincent de Paul in the charitable works he had called to life, she encounters different groups of people. The people of the Caritas clubs and the ladies of Parisian society come together for charitable causes, and eventually from a small group of committed young women develops the Company of the Daughters of Charity.

It is Louise's concern to strengthen and build up these Companies in their inner cohesion. She has to deal with communities in which people who are very different from each other come together because a common cause unites them. It is clear for her that resolution and perseverance are needed to let an inner unity come about.

Of help here are the basic attitudes of humility, simplicity, and love. To these she adds another aspect:

"If humility, simplicity and charity, which produce support, are well established among

you, your little Company will be made up of as many saints as there are persons. We must not wait, however, for someone else to begin." (L. 505)

With this enters an expression which in the context of community life is found very frequently with her: the "bearing" with one another, as she calls it. This is an expression sounding rather like a burden or inconvenience to our ears today. So, let us look at the original French text in order to be able to understand Louise well: the French word *"supporter"* means first of all "carry, support, get along with one another, tolerate something," and only then, also, "endure, suffer." Translated into today's language, Louise, therefore, means also to take others as they are, and to let them be. For her this is linked with great sensitivity towards the other and readiness to give support.

When this attitude becomes the building material for living with one another, for cooperation, trust will grow, and inner agreement becomes possible. Louise is convinced:

"In this way a spirit of unity is nourished in communities, and trust is firmly established in them for the glory of God and the sanctification of souls." (L. 394)

Reflection

◎ Where do I experience community? What is it characterized by?

◎ What is important to me personally to be able to act in a constructive manner?

4 To Make the World More Human

Making the world more human – this can in no way be accomplished on one's own. In 1625 Louise meets Vincent de Paul for the first time. From the beginning, which was not immediately "love at first sight," a resilient and fruitful journeying together develops in the coming years, fundamental for the work of both saints.

What is characteristic of this way-companionship?

There is first of all the readiness to deal with each other in great openness. Louise learns to clearly voice in front of Vincent what she recognizes as her vocation. She writes to him:

"I will hold back nothing ..., since God has always given me the grace to want you to see all my thoughts, actions and intentions as clearly as His goodness sees them." (L. 411)

Louise knows what she wants, and she knows how to express her positions and convictions with clarity – in discussions with Vincent, but also before political or Church authorities.

At the same time, it is typical for her, that she holds a certain mistrust against an excess of her own will. This reserve and the fear of wanting to extort anything, is closely linked to her own history. Often enough she had to experience in the fate of her own family members how easily power and influence can be misused.

Vincent helps her to find an inner freedom that takes clear positions and at the same time makes itself available in a listening attitude. In this way she becomes also for others a way-companion into freedom, *"since I must believe that God is the absolute Master in the direction of souls."* (A. 36)

The way-companionship of Louise and Vincent manifests not least of all in a great creativity. Both understand how to enter the experience of the other and so meet the other halfway. An example:

At times it was difficult for Vincent to answer Louise's letters in time and in detailed manner because of his workload. This gave Louise the idea, to develop a sort of questionnaire, where he only had to put a "yes" or "no" or write short notes at the margins.

Reflection

◎ Do I consider openness, request for feedback and creativity necessary for stable companionship?

◎ How does that look in the network of my relationships?

◎ How do I share the walk as a companion with others?

5 Never to Be Idle

Louise is aware that spiritual life gains its form in the actions that are borne from it. In her "Rule of life in the world" she writes:

"I shall try never to be idle. Therefore, after these few minutes of meditation, I shall work cheerfully, until four o'clock, either for the Church or for the poor or for my household ... I would strive to be particularly attentive to the Word of God and to His law expressed in His commandments." (A. 1)

Louise does not promote an agitated activism, but indicates an inner readiness to lend a hand when the situations calls for it. She writes:

"It is enough that God knows that we are all ready to work whenever He wishes." (L. 141)

This requires a healthy look at that which is possible.

"I am sure, my dear Sister, that you have a lot to do but, for the love of God, undertake only what you can accomplish." (L. 647b)

Moreover, it is clear to her that solid work can be a cure against inner afflictions:

"If you are discouraged ... then you must work. Laziness brings sin to the soul and illness to the body." (L. 565)

In this she leads by her good example – the Sisters experience her as a good superior, who is fully at the task and dauntlessly gives a hand, wherever there is something to do. She recommends this good example also to those who carry responsibility in the community – the "Sisters Servants":

Her experience has led her to see *"very clearly the difference between a Sister Servant who says, "Let's do this," and the one who is content to say, "Do this," without ever putting her hand to the task."* (L. 647b)

When the goal of our commitment is clear, our every initiative and the effort that comes with it brings joy and fulfillment. Thus, Louise asks us too:

"Is it not glorious for souls to cooperate with God in carrying out this plan?" (A. 27)

Reflection:

◎ What gives me strength for my work, what spurs me on?

◎ Who is my model and my good example?

6 Perseverance in Adversity

"Great courage and steadfastness are essential in order to persevere here because ... we are often exposed to the danger of discouragement in various circumstances." (L. 481)

Louise knows the experience of adversities and problems of normal everyday life overwhelming us. In 1649 she lives through such a phase: the civil war is intensifying, many of the hopeful beginnings do not develop as was desired, sisters are leaving the community, Vincent is on a six-month visitation trip, and so Louise has to deal with all the questions on her own.

She concentrates on what helps her to persevere. As so many other times she finds the answer looking at Jesus. Just as he took adversities upon himself, she also wants to face her problems. She writes:

"When God's spirit resides in souls, it removes the weakness ... Nothing can make us more like Jesus Christ than persecution suffered peacefully." (L. 271)

Furthermore, she recognizes that the inner confrontation with difficulties is nothing unusual on the spiritual journey:

"This does not mean that nature does not at times provide even the most perfect with occasions for struggle, but you realize that this is to test the fidelity of souls desirous of belonging completely to God. Do not be surprised then, my dear Sisters, when such a thing happens; rather this is a time when our souls must be moved, despite the weakness of our nature, to practice heroic virtue by spontaneous acts of humility and gentleness of heart and to prove that we desire to be truly Christian." (L. 447)

The commitment to be with Christ on the journey, and the willingness to anchor her heart in him, give Louise a deeply-seated serenity.

Out of this confidence she assures her sisters:

"If you can all act accordingly, you will be the bravest women in the world and I truly believe that you will be doing what God is asking of you." (L. 284)

Reflection

◎ For Louise persevering is a sign of true preparedness to follow Christ. What helps *me* in this?

◎ When I am in over my head, I look at Christ: Louise's advice to me!

7 The Gaze at Christ

In 1660 it is foreseeable that Louise is completing her mission in the world. Her health is never stable, but from February on it is clearly visible that she has entered into the last stretch of her Journey. She walks it very consciously.

When she bids her Sisters farewell she entrusts to their hearts what is most essential to her. Those who are gathered at her sickbed keep these words faithfully in their memory and write them down:

> *"My dear Sisters, I still continue to ask God for His blessing for you. I ask that He may show you the grace, to be perseverant in your vocation, so that you may serve Him in the way He desires of you.*
> *Be very thorough in the service to the poor. Before all else, live together in great unity and cordiality. Have mutual love for each other, and thus imitate the unity and the life of Our Lord. Earnestly implore the Holy Virgin that she may be your only Mother."*

As a summary, her "Spiritual Testament" still shows her sisters still today how they can walk their path in the strength of mercy. It holds important promptings for all who want to walk in the footsteps of Christ.

God comes to meet us, calls us personally and waits for our answer. This answer opens a dialogue of love between him and us. Thus, one's own vocation finds its form. For Louise it is concentrated in "service to the poor." In the reality of her life there are ever new ways to be there for others who are in need and who find the possibilities for their lives restricted. This is not always going to be easy - it is not for nothing that Louise speaks of perseverance.

Such commitment becomes possible, when people find one another in a common cause and give this community its form through cordial cooperation. To seek reciprocal understanding remains an essential duty.

The guideline and golden thread in doing so is the gaze at Christ. The desire to be more like him and to ask in the concrete everyday occurrences "what Jesus would do in my place" lets us advance on the road to follow him. Mary, who fully involved herself on this journey, will be our guide and help.

The witness of Louise's life gives an insight into the strength stemming from the depth of her faith that envelopes her whole commitment and keeps her from burning out. She takes God's love more seriously than the hard experiences of her life – in everything, she knows herself to be carried and guided and thus becomes whole from within. In this way she has given countless people the precious gift of leading them and accompanying them into friendship with God Louise can be a good way-companion for many still today.

Personally, I am certain that she takes me, too, by the hand and prays for me.

"I hope that our good God will bless the care you give, and I pray that He will grant you sufficient strength and courage to overcome the little difficulties you will encounter. I remain in His most holy love, your very humble sister and servant." (L. 43)

Biographical Data

Dec. 8, 1591 Louise is born (probably in Paris) as daughter of Louis de Marillac.

January 1595 For her schooling Louise goes to the Dominican Convent in Poissy.

1604 Louise changes school and attends the Household Management School

July 25, 1604 Her father dies.

1612 Louise asks to be admitted to the Daughters of the Passion and is rejected because of her poor health.

Feb. 5, 1613 Marriage to Antoine Le Gras at the church of St. Gervais in Paris.

Oct. 18, 1613 Birth of their only child Michel-Antoine.

June 4, 1623 "Pentecost event": Louise is led out of her inner night and finds the answer to the questions for her life.

1624 or 25 First encounter with Vincent de Paul, probably through intervention of Francis de Sales.

Dec. 21, 1625 Antoine Le Gras dies after a long illness with need for care.

1629 Commissioned by Vincent de Paul, Louise visits the rural Caritas associations.

May 1632 Her uncles, Michel and Jean Louis, meet their death in a revolt against Richelieu.

Nov. 29, 1633 Four or five young women move into Louise's apartment: Foundation of the Daughters of Charity.

March 25, 1642 Louise and four other sisters take vows.

Jan. 18, 1655 Approbation of the Daughters of Charity by the Archbishop of Paris; officially recognized by the state through King Louis XIV in 1657.

March 15, 1660 Louise dies in Paris.

May 9, 1920 Beatification.

March 11, 1934 Canonization.

Feb. 10, 1960 Declared patron of all those working in social work.

Her feast day is celebrated on May 9, the day of her beatification.

(Until 2016 it was celebrated on March 15, the day of her death.)

Also available in the same series:

Praying Advent
Three Minute Reflections on Peace, Faithfulness,
Joy, and Light
Joan Mueller
ISBN: 978-1-56548-358-3

Keepsakes for the Journey
Four Weeks on Faith Deepening
Susan Muto
ISBN: 978-1-56548-333-0

Pathways to Relationship
Four Weeks on Simplicity, Gentleness, Humility, Friendship
Robert F. Morneau
ISBN: 978-1-56548-317-0

Pathways to Community
Four Weeks on Prudence, Justice, Fortitude and Temperance
Robert F. Morneau
ISBN: 978-1-56548-303-3

Pathways to God
Four Weeks on Faith, Hope and Charity
Robert F. Morneau
ISBN: 978-1-56548-286-9

Peace of Heart
Reflections on Choices in Daily Life
Marc Foley
ISBN: 978-1-56548-293-7

To order call 1-800-462-5980
or e-mail orders@newcitypress.com